REAL CVs for
REAL PEOPLE

REAL CVs *for* REAL PEOPLE

A headhunter's guide to help intelligent people write a winning CV

Tim Chenevix-Trench

RICHDATA BOOKS

Copyright © 2012 Tim Chenevix-Trench

All rights reserved. No part of this publication may be reproduced transmitted in any form or by any means, electronic or mechanical including photocopying, recording or any information storage or retrieval system, without prior permission in writing from the publisher.

The right of Tim Chenevix-Trench to be identified as the author of this work has been asserted by him in accordance with the Copyright, Designs and Patents Act 1988

First published in the United Kingdom in 2012
by Richdata books

ISBN 978-0-9572613-0-3

Disclaimer

The views expressed in this book are those of the author, but they are general views only, and readers are urged to consult a relevant and qualified specialist for individual advice in particular situations. The author and publisher accept no responsibility for any consequences arising directly, or indirectly, from advice given herein.

Contents

Part 1	The process of creating a CV	1
Chapter 1	What this book is about, and who it is written for	2
Chapter 2	More preparatory general background	4
Chapter 3	Why do CVs matter?	6
Chapter 4	How to set about writing a CV or résumé	9
Chapter 5	Why CVs go wrong	13
Chapter 6	Different styles in different types of recruitment process	16
Chapter 7	How to start writing a CV	18
Chapter 8	Layout – general principles and opening paragraphs	23
	Detailed format, line by line	25
	Summary so far	28
	Other information	31
	Formats and layout	32
	Language and style	33
Chapter 9	Internet and formats for computer reading of CVs	40
Chapter 10	Dealing with thorny issues such as gaps in your career	42
Chapter 11	Interpreting advertisements	47
Chapter 12	Briefing on the company	48
Chapter 13	Keywords	49

Part 2   The psychological foundation for careers and CVs 51

Chapter 14   The psychological foundation for writing CVs: some basic guidelines and thoughts   52

    What is a manager?   54

    Career strategy and strategic thinking   57

    Now about yourself   58

    When you have done all this thinking   60

Chapter 15   A final summary and check list   61

Part 3   Examples of CVs and how to improve them   63

    Two very different sample CVs, on the model described   64

    Sections of real CVs before and after 'treatment'   68

ACKNOWLEDGEMENT

The contents and opinions in this book are the responsibility of the author alone.

The author wishes to express his profound thanks to Adrian Thomas, Chairman of the Recruitment Society, who has in a distinguished recruitment career worked for Network Rail and the Royal Bank of Scotland among others. Adrian has given advice from his formidable professional experience and knowledge: in general, and particularly in regard to the implications of the use of computers in automatic tracking and analysis of CVs.

Part 1

The process of creating a CV

Chapter 1

What this book is about, and who it is written for

THIS LITTLE BOOK seeks to provide stimulating and practical help to intelligent people wanting to produce a seriously good, winning CV. The aim of writing a CV is generally to get an interview: the first key step in getting a new job. The book is a guide to producing a sane and grown-up CV for presentation to competent and insightful managers. It is for use in a world where there is competition for every job and where CVs at almost any level are computer-processed. It is written by an experienced headhunter with a habit of independent thinking and steeped in practical psychology.

The people it is intended to help are across the spectrum: from senior managers to salespeople, apprentices, graduates, technicians and anyone with a profession or job needing some kind of qualification. My experience in headhunting is that senior managers seem no better than anyone else at writing an effective CV. I conclude that however intelligent they are, people tend to be too close to their own lives to see themselves and their careers and experience with cold objectivity.

The people the book is aimed at are mainly seeking jobs in business and service organisations, including central and local government, charities, NGOs, defence, NHS and other administration, the legal profession, etc. It will not cover medical, research, academic, showbiz, military and other specialist areas of work which expect particular formats. Nonetheless even in these cases the approach in this book will help produce a more effective

What this book is about, and who it is written for

CV – even if only by demonstrating a particular kind of clear and positive thinking, and considering the reader.

Nor does it cover other forms of CV such as 'notes on staff talent' as part of a business tender or brochure, or information on a performer, composer or author as part of a concert, theatre or lecture programme – the book would become too complicated. However it is *always* worth remembering that the only purpose of writing a CV is to inform, interest and excite a response. Nothing should be written without a clear understanding of the response desired.

While the immediate purpose of a CV is to get to interview, the process of writing it offers opportunities for clarifying the aims and thinking of the writer – writing a CV is a multidimensional activity. It is a document which instantly reveals much about the writer, from how much the writer has invested in himself or herself to basic character and psychological makeup.

So this book is not for those who will 'knock up a CV for you in an hour'. At any level, writing an effective, winning CV needs time and thought.

The reader may find some assertions are counter to common conventions or politically correct views. Business is tough and getting tougher. Organisations need people with positive competencies and qualities, personal and professional. See for example *First, Break All the Rules* by Marcus Buckingham and Curt Coffman.* One characteristic of successful candidates is that they think for themselves and seek original, creative and effective ways to present themselves and their work.

It is in this spirit that this book is written.

A CV or résumé is the product of a total state of mind and attitude, which will result in success or failure in getting an interview, as the first step in getting a new job.

Bonne chance.

* Marcus Buckingham and Curt Coffman, *First, Break All the Rules* (Simon & Schuster Ltd., 2001).

Chapter 2

More preparatory general background

CVS ARE TO get an interview, rather than a job, in competition with perhaps many others who want the same interview and ultimately the same job. The quality of the CV provides the only basis on which a shortlist will be selected – and most rejected – for interview.

People often think of a CV as 'just a bit of paper – it doesn't count for much because all that matters is my current job and qualifications. They'll see who I am when I go for interview.' But they won't get that interview! That attitude ignores the existence of competition.

The book does not pretend to be *the* authority on the writing and formatting of all kinds of CV. It does not pretend to offer the 'only proper approach' to CV writing. Its main focus is on CVs for UK jobs and companies. North American résumés are shorter and have a different emphasis. EC and European résumés or CVs are likewise different, and the Business Schools have formulated their own templates. However in every case the writer's attitude of mind will produce either a document which wins in competition with others, or one which loses and is binned. It is such a pity when a first-rate person produces a second-rate résumé, which denies them a real job opportunity.

So I hope this book will help people in different countries and many work and business cultures, because the same kind of effort and good thinking is needed to make any CV or résumé a winner.

The following chapters will explain how this thinking should produce new words and new ideas to describe a person – attributes, career and experience. The resulting CV should excite the candidate-writer, as well as its reader. It should help the candidate-writer get new insights into himself or herself, in terms of experiences, career and attributes; formulate career strategy; trigger the right responses in the recruiting and interviewing company; assess whether a particular job is a right next step; and consider what questions to ask in interview.

The candidate should never forget that the hiring manager opening a CV, or shaking hands at the start of an interview, will always be hoping this candidate will be the right one!

There are many glossy books on 'How to write the perfect CV'. Many try to cover all professions, levels and types of situation. Most seem to take a patronising tone, addressing people as though they have little education, capacity or will to think. I read assertions about CV writing which seem entirely questionable. Anyone is at liberty to write any kind of CV they wish, but all that does is to make my kind of CV that much more special and stand out that much more from the norms.

I've tried to keep this book simple, deep in its psychological foundations and stimulating to people who can and want to think.

When I worked for a leading international headhunting company, each partner had perhaps 150 CVs to read in a week. We took probably five seconds on each. We knew the companies and jobs. That's all it took to know who to be interested in and who was just not of interest. I used to reckon that of that 150, perhaps three were kept as of possible interest: Would David be interested in him? Might client YYY find him a good candidate? Or: Put him on the files, I must remember him. That means 98% were rejected, binned.

It might sound unprofessional, haphazard. In fact it was the opposite. A CV speaks volumes about the writer, seen at a glance. The chapters which follow analyse how this can be so and offer ideas on how to prepare and present a CV which will fulfil its purpose.

Chapter 3

Why do CVs matter?

WHEN ANYONE WANTS a new job – as chief executive, medical consultant, salesperson, graduate trainee or local council groundsman – the first step to getting it is presenting a CV to get an interview. And the CV is often the sole basis on which an interview is offered, a decision made by a recruiter or a computer.

Depending on the level and type of the job, there may be anything from one to a hundred other people wanting that same job and competing for it. There might be 50–100 applicants for a middle management job, whether the job is advertised, headhunted or listed on the web. Of these perhaps five will be selected for interview and one will be chosen. Of all those wannabe applicants, all but five will be rejected solely on the basis of their CVs or résumés.

All those whose CVs failed will have wasted their time and lost the job opportunity: will have shot themselves and their careers in the foot.

The person who reads each CV may be highly trained or completely untrained in interpreting them. This person – referred to below as The Reader – may be entirely focused on the task of selecting candidates for interview, or may be giving a scrappy five minutes here and there over a few days to casting an eye over a hundred CVs and picking out five for interview. The Reader may be

a headhunter
an agency
a research company

- an in-company recruiter
- an employer manager
- the secretary or assistant of an employing manager
- a consultant
- a computer

While the main aim of the CV is to get an interview, obviously a really good CV can have a big impact in the post-interview stages. A superbly written and presented CV can influence the whole subsequent selection decision process. Several people are likely to be involved in the selection process and all may be influenced by the quality of a candidate's CV.

It is now the case that between 80 and 90% of big-organisation jobs are filled without an agency being involved: in other words CVs sent in directly are unfiltered before they reach the target company and are based on individual candidates' CV efforts.

One concept currently discussed in the context of CVs and job applications is the investment someone has made in himself or herself. Even at the lowest levels, at today's values, someone will earn £1m in a lifetime. A top manager will earn from £5–100m or more. Apart from the traditional education and basic training, has the CV writer made any imaginative or dynamic efforts to increase his or her earning power, level, capabilities, skills, social position, influence …? Some people do in fact take remarkable initiatives. The following is an anodised extract from a recent CV of a candidate I was privileged to interview:

> Left school at 16, did apprenticeship with xxx. 1st hons Electrical Engineering degree in 1998. In his first management job with [big consulting firm] he decided to broaden himself and started a ten-year programme to broaden his expertise. Enrolled on an Engineering Management Partnership course run by B..., B... & L... Universities; after completing this opted to go for a full PhD. Completed courses on leadership in engineering as preparation for the PhD, then courses on corporate finance, HR management and

behavioural studies, marketing, corporate social responsibility, ICT, leadership and team building ... Completed the PhD in 20xx, with thesis 'Improving infrastructure projects in the heavy xxx industry' – conducted entirely by himself in his own time with company financial support. Last 7–8 years dominated by his studies.

Chapter 4

How to set about writing a CV or resumé

THE CV IS LIKELY to be the only thought-out piece of written work from the candidate that the selectors will see at any time before making their final choice of successful candidate.

I've been a headhunter for 25 years. People often ask me how to write a CV. I reply that a CV should take 20–30 hours of work. Why?

It has to be more relevant and interesting than the competitors, perhaps all 100 of them. If it isn't and is binned with most of the others, it will exclude the writer from the job.

The process of writing a CV should teach the writer what ideas and words to use about himself/herself. Remember that describing a new product can take a professional marketing manager weeks of work.

A well-written and well-presented CV will have many qualities which set it apart and make the writer look really interesting; achieving this requires intense concentration and refinement.

Preliminary requirements for a good CV are:

a genuine and passionate wish to get an interview and a job,
recognition that there will be intense competition for both,
being prepared to take immense care in preparing the CV,
approaching the task with an interested, positive attitude.

Shoving a hundred casually or shoddily written CVs into the post, or launching them into the internet ether, will be a waste of time, effort and money.

A winning CV is about the writer, his or her attributes and their relevance to the job applied for. It is not about the writer's current or past jobs. (If you don't see the difference you shouldn't be reading this.) A winning CV will communicate the writer's

- Relevance to the job, the company and its business
- Professional substance
- Professional and personal achievement
- Level of investment in himself/herself
- Spark, and how interesting he/she is
- Substance of personality, style, values and vitality
- Balance and strength of personality
- Ability to take responsibility, in other words what has been entrusted to the writer in personal and professional life
- Conciseness and clarity of thinking and presentation
- Maturity
- Quality of mind
- Emotional intelligence
- Forward-looking approach
- Understanding of how to communicate effectively

A good headhunter or recruiter reading a CV can see what there is of most of these in seconds – and as quickly can see shoddy thinking, poor design, lack of sincerity, wishful thinking, poor accuracy, mindless comments about the writer's abilities and qualities ...

There are no short cuts to producing a winning CV (though of course there will be a gifted few who will get it right first time!).

Many people want a quick ready-made CV formula or template. Many pay a company to write their CV for them. These approaches seldom produce good results. The resulting CVs generally have an instantly visible quality marking them out as second-rate. It seems to me essential that each person produces his or her own CV if it is to show the required effort and depth of insight.

If someone else writes it, unless they know you well, it will not in general get the same concentrated and informed thought; it will usually be in a standardised format, and it will fail to reflect the personality and values of the candidate – through the strange magic of words chosen by the writer. In other words it will become a document written by a committee of two. Moreover if the CV is written by someone else, the candidate will not have buy-in and this will always show up in an interview. Why ask *anyone* else to portray your skills and experience?

Should you have and use a standard CV, or tailor-make one for each application?

There is a temptation in writing this kind of book to make a rule for every situation and question. I felt this would make the book too complicated. A person seeking a job really must make up his/her own mind about this.

My observations would be:

> For any job you really want, and for all jobs at senior level, do a version tailored for that job, that company and that organisation. The current post-recession job markets are ruthless in their demand for a 'perfect application'.
>
> Have a superb general-purpose CV meeting the standards set in this book. Tweak it for most job applications; there may not be time to make it significantly different for each of, say, 50–100 applications.
>
> Do make a significant effort to write a tailored version when applying to a new industry or new sector, for example if moving from fashion to construction; highlight transferable skills. The most important comments in this situation will, however, be made in the covering letter.

Transferring between sectors is often important. Sectors offering the most opportunity are always changing. It is obvious today that healthcare, local and central government, energy, financial services, transport and branches of engineering offer a growing number of opportunities for careers and progression. Correspondingly, in other sectors jobs will never return. People from these will have to move to new sectors, and the above comments will be of real importance.

A lot of personal judgement is needed to assess when and whether it is worth applying for jobs in different sectors. In this, as in so many matters, there are no rules nowadays. An inspirational approach by an individual will succeed where a dozen more boring approaches will fail. This is discussed further in the later section 'Psychological foundations for careers and CVs'.

The whole area of skills transfer is little understood by HR people or hiring managers. A dynamic and well-thought-out few lines in a CV and accompanying letter, combined with a bit of homework about the target sector, can often work wonders and excite the hiring firm.

Chapter 5

Why CVs go wrong

Let's get some big negatives out of the way. Some commonly made mistaken approaches are instantly observable and are instant turnoffs.

People want to *talk about themselves*. They load (or pad out) their CV with detail of no interest to anyone. They *don't stop to think about what The Reader wants to know* about them. They forget that a reader is uninterested in anything they've done except insofar as it shows that the writer may be able to solve The Reader's business problems in the future. A discursive, boring CV will be binned.

People do not consider how to *design a document* that will have the impact needed to make it read and understood. A CV with narrow margins, countless words crammed into a page, and bullet points by the score, places a demand on mind and time which no normal busy person will bother with. It also reveals a corresponding style of work and communication which no hiring manager wants. A shabby CV will be binned.

CV writers forget the first rule of communication: that what is *communicated is not what is said but what is heard; not what is written but what is read and taken in* – this is an extension of the comments in the previous paragraph. A thoughtless CV will be binned.

CVs full of acronyms or jargon, as well as those with mistakes in spelling and punctuation, do more to put The Reader off than their writers could imagine. Irritation leads to the bin!

CV writers rarely stop to think about *who and what they really are* with cold objectivity, as products relevant to the market in which they are selling themselves. They rarely present information about themselves in a balanced and concise way. A mindless CV will be binned.

CV writers who list or 'summarise' their own attributes and achievements do not realise that the person reading their CV can instantly see what is fiction and wishful thinking: can spot a crude attempt to sell the writer as full of virtues which are patently imaginary. A pompous, wishful-thinking or deceitful CV will be binned.

Having read thousands of CVs, I literally cannot bring myself to read comments by the writers about themselves. Most such comments are empty, wishful-thinking words to sell the writer, usually simple untruths. Most just make the writer look pathetic. When in an interview I ask a manager about his or her style, and get the reply 'firm but fair', I want to show the interviewee the door: it is so mindless and trite.

Examples from real CVs are:

'An individual that shapes and delivers strategy, with an emphasis on execution and through leading and motivating large multi-functional teams'.

'An accomplished executive and published author with 15 years of experience in business operations and technology development with a subspecialty in applications deployment CRM and CM. Reputation for quality and innovative ideas, fostering opportunity-rich relationships, self-motivation and commitment to achieving ambitious, yet attainable goals.'

'I can work either alone or as part of a team. I am accurate and precise. I am able to communicate effectively to a wide audience and am able to apply logic and analysis skills to a variety of work-based situations.'

'Excellent Communication skills, Professional and Diligent approach to Tasks.'

Why CVs go wrong

'Expert in risk management and management control solutions, with particular experience in delivering projects relating to contract management and acquisition due diligence. Able to work at all levels in a variety of commercial sectors, from basic individual tasks to leadership of highly qualified project teams on complex issues.'

'An accomplished and highly experienced senior commercial manager with a proven track record spanning 20 years in a UK & Pan European business to business and business to consumer service industry.'

'I am an experienced manager...'

In the same way, a long list of achievements at the front of a CV simply doesn't help. Such a list double guesses – always wrongly – what The Reader wants to know, and is irrelevant. And it does not, for example, tell The Reader in which job or phase of a career each achievement happened.

The hiring recruiter/manager/reader wants to know everything *quickly, concisely, accurately and clearly.* All subjective messages about special personal qualities, leadership ability, values, things the writer thinks are important, must emerge from the factual text – then they become believable. Such is the magic of words.

Chapter 6

Different styles in different types of recruitment process

EACH LEVEL AND TYPE of job application calls for a different approach to achieve the desired result: an interview. Examples:

The top level appointment – for example for chairman or non-executive director or multinational board member:

This is likely to be one page supported by 2-3 pages of carefully selected detail put together for each job applied for. At this level the professional reader can be expected already to know the person – or at least a lot about him or her. At this level also the individual is likely to be headhunted. Even so his CV can be critical: a poor one can be off-putting to the hiring chairman, CEO or board.

Director or senior manager:

Of a business, local or national government organisation, national government position, charity, NGO, university, museum etc. A 2- or possibly 3-page CV is expected, along the lines proposed in this book.

Academic, medical etc:

Will vary depending on level; standard formats are expected which will include detailed listing of publications, research etc and can run to many pages.

Salespeople, administration, technical, engineering, local government etc:

Jobs normally with qualifications required. A carefully written 2-page CV following the guidelines below, unless a specific format is demanded by the recruiter.

Different styles in different types of recruitment process

Mass recruitment:

Nowadays is often computer-based with computer selection techniques, requiring specific formats and with keywords according to recruiter specifications.

In every case, as the basis for success, the CV or résumé must somehow communicate the generic personal and professional qualities sought by hiring managers and recruiters.

These qualities and competencies must somehow emerge from the words used and must be visible in every version of the CV sent out. We will talk abut how to achieve this.

Whether or not hiring managers feel that directly relevant experience is strictly necessary, in almost all cases they will want to find a generic level of quality and ability: the right level of professional experience, the right attitude and the right personal qualities. Such personal qualities must shine through the CV as the career story unfolds.

Chapter 7

How to start writing a CV

It is my opinion that *with enough effort and care*, the CV of any accomplished manager, admiral of the fleet, museum director or research scientist can be written within two pages. Extra information such as publications or research, where this is relevant, or the extra ground covered by, for example, a dual career, may extend this to three pages.

There will be circumstances in which a longer document is called for, for example:

Once a top manager has been selected for interview

Medical and specialist CVs, with a long list of technical detail

R&D or academic CVs where technical details are required

IT technical CVs: here a short CV followed by technical detail is in my opinion the most effective – unless a specific format is requested, or unless a purely technical cv is appropriate with no human qualities required.

However, a 'normal' CV which extends beyond two pages, in my opinion:

has failed to devote enough effort to creating that crystal clear winning document – in itself a damning feature;

expects The Reader to be interested in – or grapple with – what the writer wants to say, over and beyond what The Reader needs to know to decide whether or not interview;

fails to acknowledge time and mind pressure on The Reader;

may actually conceal key information under other information not needed for the decision whether or not to interview (see Example 4 at the end of the book).

One good starting approach is to sit down and write 10-20 pages about yourself, your career and your achievements. Then steadily whittle that down to two pages expressing twice as much as in the original. Strangely that is always possible. But it takes many hours of work – and an attitude of mind prepared to *cut out all the pet words and previously conceived favourite ideas about yourself* – a fundamental requirement of the best writing.

In this, as in doing a job and in being selected for a job, 'attitude' is everything!

Every single word in a CV counts and must be made to count. Every space, letter, line must be used to good effect. This will be seen in the detailed formatting described below and in the examples given at the end. The final stages of cutting out spare spaces, lines, letters and words can take hours.

Earlier it was observed that the process of writing a CV teaches you what words to use about yourself, how to describe yourself as a product for sale. Early in the process of preparing a CV, it is fruitful to write four, perhaps five, short summary statements about yourself which between them encapsulate what you are, your area of experience, personal characteristics and what you want.

These *must* be verifiable statements of fact (not wishful thinking). If they are accurate, striking and strong enough, they should go near the top of the CV in 4 or 5 lines of bold, large font in italics. Use a clear, modern font such as Verdana. Creating these abbreviated statements can take many hours; you can mull them around in the back of your mind for days. They should crystallise to The Reader instantly exactly what you are. They can also provide a useful 'relevance thread' as the CV progresses.

Some examples:

General manager in multinational automotive & hitech
High integrity leader; attracts, retains top international talent
Expands boundaries in people, cultures, new business, strategy
Manages strategic customer relationships
Business experience across Europe, USA, Latin America, China

Vice Admiral, Deputy Commander-in-Chief Fleet
Leader-manager, exceptional people skills, independent mind
Able to take strategic & difficult decisions; tested in war
Nuclear submarine commander at 35
At 56, seeking a new career and new life challenges

Created & directed world's leading industry-university programme
In parallel created & ran a successful media business
Huge personal dynamic, integrity, 'make it happen'
At 55 ready for new career: marketing? –
international talent sourcing? – customer relations director?

Ambitious and motivated final year undergraduate
Leadership skills proved in varied & demanding work experience
Widely informed: from politics and sport to the law
Revels in creative problem-solving and challenges

Commercial new media director with massive experience
Track record of international business development, sales, negotiation
High-integrity leader and motivator of teams
Dynamic, passionate creator of leading-edge business

How to start writing a CV

Proven, successful CEO of a $300m US publishing business
International M, A, D & restructuring experience*
In media and new media since Web1.0
Now plans to return to Europe

Golf Professional 5 years, leading club officer
Runs golf shop, organises club activities, IT, budgets
Teaching, looks after visitors and members
Represents club to press and public

An important part of the attitude in sitting down to write the CV is that it should be forward looking. Nothing you've done is of any interest to The Reader except insofar as it shows you can solve his problems in the future. It's always worth saying – concisely – what your intended career next step, hope, objective, ambition, aims etc are. Ensure that what you say is in tune with the job application for which you are using the CV.

In this context, the CV should display how you have grown, matured, acquired new skills, been given new and bigger responsibilities, and achieved greater successes – demonstrating growth and steady development.

Always avoid detail which readers do not need to know. If they are interested they will find out the detail they want, when they want it. For a middle-level job or above, no employer at this stage wants to know where you went to school, what GCSEs you got, all the training courses you've done. One exception is the specific date you joined and left each of your jobs. Banking, much of government and security firms etc require positive vetting of any gap of more than two to three weeks, supported by documented evidence of the cause of the gap.

---

* M, A, D will be known as mergers, acquisitions and disposals by anyone to whom the CV is relevant. Clear and generally accepted abbreviations reduce words and valuable space; in this particular case it allows the information to fit into one line with huge impact.

As with so much of the substance of this book about writing CVs, if you don't know – i.e. don't take the trouble to work out – what to leave out or put in, you won't get it right! And it will show the recruiter/Reader that you don't know. And because not knowing is a sure sign of professional immaturity, your CV will be binned.

Chapter 8

Layout – general principles and opening paragraphs

AT THIS POINT a new theme needs to be introduced. It is of making this an interesting document which is a pleasure to read.

It has got to look better than all the other CVs The Reader will see. The Reader must be made to sit up and feel good and positive about it the moment he or she sees it.

Never forget that the moment The Reader opens up your CV or welcomes you into his or her office, he or she hopes you will be the person they need. You wouldn't be there otherwise.

Firstly, this document is about *you*. The CV is the one time that, bluntly, you are out there selling yourself against competitors who are also selling themselves – like crazy. If you don't enter into the selling spirit, you will lose (to better salespeople who may otherwise be far less qualified then you). Therefore use the 'I' word. Don't ever refer to yourself in the third person. It looks stilted and pathetic.

For most conventional CV situations the layout described in the following pages appears to me to be the 'best'. Best because it

- is concise, in a way that displays what is strategically important about you and your attributes;
- eliminates information/words of no interest to The Reader;
- is immediately, visually, digestable and understandable;
- communicates who and what you are up front;
- enables The Reader to make instant phone or email contact.

Clearly there can be no absolute 'best', but I have not found a more effective layout or approach.

In my opinion the politically correct dogma which says no one should include age, sex, marital status etc is misguided. Any employer wants to know these things, the more so the more senior the position. If the recruiter is ageist or has other prejudices he will find ways to avoid employing you anyway. The moral fault in allowing prejudice to determine recruitment lies with the recruiter and employer, not with the person applying for a job.

Of course most of it will become clear at interview; things like age can be worked out roughly from the CV – unless you leave out early career jobs which can be seen as lying to create a deliberately false impression.

If anything, to me the failure to state age means that someone is probably trying to hide his or her age and is therefore afraid of it. I don't want someone who is afraid to face up to something as basic as their own age. Recruiters are looking for real people. It is good to know someone's family situation – for example in a job with a lot of travel I would consider it essential to know this.

Some people will say that after getting 20 rejections, any trick is worth playing to get in front of a potential employer, and perhaps to bypass the prejudice of the intermediate agency recruiter. What can one say?

Political correctness practised in the wrong way seems to me a cult of fear. I don't want fearful people. Appointing ineffective people who cannot cope with the real world, who will then lose the job and have to be replaced, will cost me and the business too much time, money and lost opportunity.

Detailed format, line by line

Don't put Curriculum Vitae at the top. It is wasted space; everyone knows what the document is.

Top line: in large bold print

Name centred

Then on one line: in smaller font

Address, phone(s), email, website: don't put 'tel', 'mobile', 'email' etc – it's obvious what they are

Then on one line: in smaller font

Nationality; DoB 3rd Jan 1965 (46), married, 3 children

Note: add nationality only if the reader might think you do not have the necesary work permits or residency, or if the job is in a multicultural organisation

Then in 4–5 lines: in larger font

The heavy type 4–5-line summary described above

Then: heading in bold larger print

Education, qualifications

Then: ordinary small type

One line: first degree, e.g. BA, BSc or other first qualification, honours level, year completed, university

BSc (2.1) Electrical & Electronic Engineering 1984, Hertfordshire University

Then: ordinary small type

Second degree, e.g. PhD with subject of thesis, one line if possible here (you can give the full title in the career section)

PhD, Nottingham University 2006 (thesis on brain simulation)

Then: ordinary small type

One line, abbreviated other qualifications. Special levels and achievements should have a date, e.g. FCIS 1999 or FIET 2007

ChEng, EurIng, ACIS, FIET (2008)

Then: ordinary small type

Exceptional training or other educational experience should be listed, e.g.:

2008 Advanced Management Achievement Course, Manchester BS
2006 Senior Managers' Financial Seminar, London BS
2005 Revolution in Business Practices (US DoD top strategic course)
1997 MoD top command course
1995 Joint Services Defence College (=MSc level strategic studies)
1977 Graduate from Dartmouth (1st Degree level), Queen's Sword.

Other training, internal and external, should be summarised as, e.g.:

Extensive training: project/programme management, people management, behavioural psychology, accounting, risk management

Or

Extensive and advanced sales-related training, account management etc

Or if no other training or qualifications

5 GCSEs, C&Guilds 1 & 111 Electrical Engineering (2 distinctions)
HNC and apprenticeship, mechanical engineering; extensive training: project management, people management

If you only have A levels it can be worth listing them. Otherwise I don't think it is necessary to put in exam subjects at any level below degree, HNC, HND etc: just the number of subjects at each level: e.g.

3 As, 14 Os, 7 GCSEs.

That's all The Reader needs to know. Are you a gardener, a rocket scientist or brain surgeon?

Then: heading in bold larger print

Personal

A section (in ordinary small type) which should be short, factual, supportable with evidence, and gives exceptional personal achievements and interests, e.g.:

Layout – general principles and opening paragraphs

I have run two careers in parallel: one in a hitech multinational, from sales to creating the world's leading industry-university program; the other in local radio as Chairman, owner and presenter. The first developed my selling, negotiating, consulting & problem-solving skills; the second honed my action, business & marketing skills, and skill in presentation & managing 'creative' people. I build high-trust business relationships across cultures. Interests: radio, music, record collecting, fishing, theatre, jogging. I have travelled worldwide, can travel.

Or:

My career has given me rare and international experience: in command, operational planning & management, advice at ministerial level, big project management, large budgets, negotiation and diplomacy, and strategic thinking aimed at <u>winning</u>.

My search for new challenges could take me in several directions: e.g. national functions, large projects, marine operations, or non-executive board positions. I bring exceptional personal & professional qualities, competencies, analytical skills, open mindedness and sense of strategy.

Or, following 'interests':

Olympic gold medalist in Shooting; Member of British Athletes Commission, still coach the British team; golf (h/c 7); fly fishing; keeping fit; family.

Summary so far:

By the time The Reader has got one third of the way down the first page he or she will know a lot about you, such as:

> Who you are,
> where you live,
> how to contact you,
> whether you are a family person,
> how broad your interests are,
> how much you have invested in yourself,
> Whether you have any exceptional personal qualities or achievements,
> Whether you are a leader,
> Whether you are a people manager,
> Whether you have international experience,
> Whether you can travel,
> Whether you are qualified,
> how academically bright and accomplished you are,
> with what clarity you can describe your abilities,
> Whether you have done interesting/demanding personal/professional development and training,
> how much energy and initiative you have,
> Whether you are afraid of your age or not having qualifications,
> you are a straightforward and outgoing person,
> how positively you see yourself,
> whether you are a whinger …

If you've created a good impact by the end of the first third of the first page, good!

Then comes: heading in bold larger print

Career information

Now for the story of your career. Because you *must make it a story*, well told with spark and precision. Not a word too many, accurate, concise, showing what responsibility you have been given or earned, what battles you have fought, where you have won, how you add value, how you have developed ... This story is where your mental ability to express your work history and to pick out formative and dynamic information will be most tested.

The norm is to list your jobs held in reverse order, current or latest job first. It is important to express the story in a way that allows The Reader to see clearly how you have developed.

You want to make it boring? Then use bullet points. The more bullet points and silly little different kinds of bullet point symbols you use, the worse the effect. No busy manager has the time or mental energy to take in a list of the things you have done or that you can't be bothered to prioritise into a single sentence. Bullet points equal boredom equals the bin.

Start each employing company with the specific dates you joined and left, and a 1–2-line summary of the company's business including the scale in £/$, sector and indicating whether it is multinational. It can be appropriate to include the websites of these companies, and at the end the websites of companies you are particularly interested in for the computer to pick up.

For example:

> 21/3/2001 **The Fourth Space Ltd**
> –9/9/2003 Large health and leisure centre in central London. Smaller font

Or

> 5/9/1980   **Highscale Instruments**
> – current $8bn semiconductors and electronics multinational

Then the job details preceded by the date. Intermediate sized font

> 1987–94   Japanese Business Manager (Europe). Championed the need for, and given responsibility for, Semiconductor Sales to Japanese & Far Eastern companies operating in Europe.

	Hired and supervised a sales team of 12 across Europe and in Japan. Learned I could manage people from varied cultures. Built the business from $1-25m, then managed its restructuring out into the sector organisation.
1980–87	Technical Sales Engineer then Sales Manager in Automotive, Consumer, Home Computer and Industrial Markets. Wonderful varied market experience. Highlights: getting an MCU designed into the Ford Sierra, display drivers into Jaguar XJ6. Recruited and developed people who became XXXX EMEA Directors.

Or another example:

1995	Returned to Germany in 1991 to take over the European Automotive Products business: the first European in the sector with P&L. I expanded our customer and product base, and created for xxxxx a strong acknowledged market position in European automotive electronics against the established European market leaders, meeting heavy prejudice as an American newcomer. The basis for this success was acquisition (& retention) of key talents from the industry; customer focused strategy; excellence in project execution; and customer intimacy. Appointed Vice President and member of the European Management Board. The global expansion of xxxxx gave me the opportunity to spearhead activities/investments in China. We established a JV in Shanghai to manufacture automotive electronic products in Taining. In 2003 xxxxx achieved its first system win for fuel injection in China.

It is sensible to reduce the level of detail given in early career jobs, but not to eliminate key formative happenings such as development of selling skills, growth in people management skills and experience, new international responsibilities, moves into project management or major promotions following new qualifications. All jobs held should be included.

Personal attributes and virtues should emerge from the facts. The above examples show this: they show positive thinking, initiative, upbeat attitudes, people skills, a sense of learning and personal development, the ability to triumph over prejudice and win people over, the ability to work successfully across different cultures and global attitudes, strategic skills, taking major initiatives and so forth.

These excerpts show conciseness and clarity of thinking. The writers are clearly not bores; their way of communicating is effective, sharp and punchy; they are achievers, and not people who want tediously to talk about their points of view and achievements.

If you have left a position in recent weeks, then in order not to be ambiguous about whether you are still in employment, put the date of employment as

3/8/2009
– 7/07/2011

It is important not to be ambiguous about whether you are still in employment. Such ambiguity comes over as dishonest.

Other information

In the course of writing this section of the CV about your work history and experience, you may have other comments to increase the interest of your experience, for example:

> Make mention of organisations you have worked for which have particular quality: for example major commercial success, massive change due to mergers or acquisitions, taking market leadership, going international, possessing internal work cultures with demanding behaviours, or high quality values;
>
> Do justice to your own work where it can be described by words such as worldwide, multicultural, mutlifunctional, market-leading technology, leading multidiscipline teams, leading teams located in many sites or countries, high-pace work culture etc;
>
> Point out roles crucial to your personal or career development.

If there is space, and if the information is significant enough, further information can be added at the end: for example special sporting achievements, awards received, special family situations, unusual interests and accomplishments.

Formats and layout

It will be remembered that the aim is for the CV to be seen and scanned by a reader in a few seconds; if it appears to be of quality, interesting and relevant – in other words *different* from the rest – then invariably The Reader will stop and read it closely to see if it is one that should be set aside for interview.

Of course the computer will also read it in the same few seconds!

Here are some suggested guidelines on visual layout and graphic design

1. Have *wide margins* all round
2. *Do not cram words into the space*: just keep the words small in number and big in impact
3. *Use a modern font*. To me, Times New Roman is old fashioned. We all have our favourites: mine is Verdana. Ariel is also generally used. Go for visual clarity – and avoid exotic fonts which Optical Character Readers may find hard to read.
4. *Vary the size of font* and use of *italic* and **bold** with skill and care. Use them to achieve impact for significant words, and reduction of space used for blocks of words. Avoid using too large or too small a font: in Verdana I would never use a larger font size than 12 or smaller than 10, with most of the words being in 11.
5. *Never use blocking*, lines around pages, boxes etc. It's corny and unsophisticated. In addition it is not appreciated by the computer, and results in larger file sizes for the recruiter to email. Keep it simple: both visually and to enable the recipient of the CV to work on it. As a headhunter I will always wish to change a CV before interview and sending it to a client; some lines and boxes can be the devil to eliminate and waste my time.
6. There's debate about use of *PDF, Word or other formats*.

Layout – general principles and opening paragraphs

Personally I find PDF CVs irritating as they are awkward to modify, and I always prefer Word. This, however, applies at more senior levels where there is a professional intermediary such as a head-hunter. At lower and more technical levels where the CV is to go straight to the company, or perhaps via an agency, a PDF may ensure correct delivery of format and a complete document.

Note that all previous changes to a Word document originated by someone else, sent out without accepting the changes, will carry the information about the document's originator and the changes made.

7   Always remember to insert a page break at the end of each page. Some recipients of electronic documents will not always produce a properly formatted document, and some will still produce a printed version in the company's own font with different spacing.

8   Most CVs will be sent by email, both from the writer to the company, and by the recruiter in the agency or company. This has the following implications:

>   All the more care is needed to ensure that a printed version will come out looking good;

>   Do not put photos or logos on the CV as this increases the file size so much that the recruiter may either have to delete the photo or logo, or split several CVs into groups to send, which is irritating.

Job ads may direct applicants to email a CV to their company, or visit their website and submit a résumé in electronic format.

Language and style

In my opinion the essence of writing a CV is to tell a story in as positive, punchy and concise a way as possible. To do this needs skill with words combined with relentless hard work and concentration.

Find the right words to describe your experience and achievements: focus on the words which tell the important information and not those which are irrelevant. Avoid the use of abstract words.

Avoid using verbs ending in –ing: use direct transitive verbs wherever possible to give sense of reality. For example

    Manage strategic customer relationships, *not*

    Managing strategic customer relationships,

    Run golf shop, organise club activities, *not*

    Running golf shop, organising club activities

Use compact language leaving out unnecessary words, to force focus on the bare facts you want The Reader to absorb.

Spend hours eliminating every unnecessary word, space, line.

And for goodness' sake *eliminate all spelling errors and mistakes* from the CV. To write 'dictionery', or 'complimentary' in the wrong context, or 'practice' as a verb, will make any educated reader cringe. Before the recession and the current tough job markets, odd spelling, format and the other errors would not necessarily doom a CV. Now errors are no longer tolerated, and the CV must be fine-tuned and proofread with the utmost care.

Layout – general principles and opening paragraphs   35

Here are two examples where sections from real CVs have been rewritten to achieve a better, more concise and more effectively communicating result.

Example 1

Original version:

1996–98 Senior Product Manager. Following success with DPN-100 up to 1996, I was promoted & built a team of 6 product managers to market large parts of the Nortel data portfolio. The team's responsibilities included Sales training, Collateral, Sales Eng. training, product positioning, pricing, customer presentations. The team were also responsible for the support of technical sales activities.

The portfolio managed included Nortel Rapport (a Dial Access product), Passport IP VPN, Multimedia Access Switch and many X.25 and Frame Relay Capabilities.

Shorter version:

1996–98 Senior Product Manager, promoted after previous success. Assembled & led a team of 6 product managers to market Nortel's core data products: Rapport, Passport IP VPN, Multimedia Access Switch, X25, Frame Relay. Activities included pricing, product positioning, sales training, collateral, customer presentations and technical support to sales.

Original was 82 words, 11 lines
Shorter version is 49 words, 6 lines

Example 2

Original version:

2000
– present
Director of Network Service Design, responsible for managing new products and technologies into COLT pan European network ensuring product needs and operational capabilities were suitably matched. Gained experience of the operational issues facing an Operator in deploying new technologies.

Currently responsible for the complete COLT 3-Year Network Strategy, defining operational models for new product and technologies and managing how future technologies will benefit or disrupt COLT.

He is an individual contributor within COLT and delivers on his responsibilities through building and managing virtual teams across Europe. Initiatives and use of virtual teams include the following:

> Leads a Virtual team of 15 people in defining and documenting the COLT 3 Year Network Strategy.

> Led Network Service Design team 2002-2003 to manage the smooth migration of new products concept from marketing into Engineering and Operations. These have included Ethernet Private Wire, Managed Security Services, IP Telephony and Voice VPNs

> Led analysis work-stream and established a supplier for an Outsourced Help Desk

> Was Build Manager in defining a trading model between COLT Internet and COLT Telecom

> Led a virtual team with responsibility for operational readiness for Secure IP-VPN Product to meet launch time of 3 months including selection of network systems suppliers. Following this Peter was asked to

Example 2 continued

>manage improvement plans for other COLT VPN products

>Led new product introduction team to operationally introduced Pan European High Capacity Services with direct involvement on sales to first customer, Dante.

New role is roughly as follows with some things to be added.

>Specify the framework (methodology and deliverables) for a development of Product Technology Programs with the aim to investigate current status and future evolution of the technology and its applicability to COLT focusing on the product aspects. These programs must include a future view of next three years.

>Drive the development of the following four Product Technology Programs using assigned resources within Product Engineering and the rest of COLT:

>>FMC applications

>>SIP based applications

>>Ethernet/optical applications

>>Low cost access

>Open programs with Universities and research centres for each of the four programs mentioned above

>Manage the introduction of low cost CPE from a Chinese supplier

>Manage relations with WiMAX forum, FMC alliance and Metro Ethernet Forum

>Complete three proof-of-concept trials for WiMAX as a fixed access method and plan for mobility through 802.16e

Example 2 continued

Search the technology market looking for the technology and applications that could be interesting for COLT in the future. This work must be presented in a quarterly document.

Develop a Mobile Offer that COLT can offer its customer in

preparation for FMC

Shorter version:

2000 – present   Director of Network Service Design reporting to Board Director

Responsible for COLT 3-Year network strategy, assessing risk and potential of new technologies, and managing their integration into operational product. I achieve this by leading virtual teams, on:

Defining and documenting COLT 3-year network product strategy (team of 15 from many EMEA countries);

Managing new network product development from concept into marketing, engineering and operations (Ethernet Private Wire, Managed Security, IP Telephony, VPNs);

Supplier selection for an outsourced Help Desk;

Defining an Internet-Telecom trading model;

Achieving operational readiness for a major secure IP-VPN product (given launch time of 3 months including selection of network systems suppliers);

Managing improvement plans for other VPN products;

Operational introduction of pan-European High Capacity Services, directly involved in the sale to first customer.

Layout – general principles and opening paragraphs 39

Example 2 continued

Gained deep experience of operational issues in deploying new network products and technologies.

My role is developing into new directions:

Extend the product and commercial assessment of new technologies across the whole product range; search for new technologies, present on these quarterly;

Drive the development of FMC, SIP, ethernet/optical and low-cost access applications: manage resources, open programmes with universities & R&D centres;

Manage introduction of China-sourced low-cost CPE;

Manage relations with WiMAX forum, FMC alliance and Metro Ethernet Forum; complete proof-of-concept trials for WiMAX as fixed access, plan for mobility;

Develop a mobile offering in preparation for FMC.

Original was 425 words, 73 lines

Shorter version is 233 words, 44 lines

Chapter 9

Internet and formats for computer reading of CVs

THIS IS COVERED in detail at various points throughout the book. To summarise the important issues:

Almost all (in numerical % terms) CVs will nowadays be computer processed: whether to track them through the recruitment process, find the candidate by data mining, or use keyword analysis for preliminary rejection of the first 30%.

CVs must use fonts clear to optical character reading.

Lines and shading are not appropriate.

Advice is generally to use Word and avoid PDF, unless an advertisement specifies a particular template or format.

Almost all CVs will be emailed: logos or photos can increase file size too much for a CV to be included in a batch, and this is irritating to the recruiter.

Also see the later section on Keywords. If the text of the CV does not confirm each Killer Question answer the computer will reject the CV.

It must also be noted that as part of the changing world, the internet is affecting most aspects of how people get jobs. One result is that recruiting and line managers get an enormously increased number of CVs. Not only will these increasingly be sifted by computer, but also the sheer quality of CVs – the absence of errors, spelling mistakes and other minor irritants – will make the selection process ever more important.

Social networking sites and their use in finding and promoting job opportunities are exploding. Subtleties in communicating through these media need to be considered with care. As with the other aspects of CV writing discussed in the rest of this book, the key is to *think*: what are the most effective words and ideas to use when I go online?

Chapter 10

Dealing with thorny issues such as gaps in your career

THIS CAN BE DIFFICULT. Stability of employment and the stability of personality which it implies are important to employers. Stability does not mean staying in the same place for all of your career: there is a balance between annual job hopping (unstable) and being in the same firm for too long (dull, lacking ambition, fear of change, narrow experience of businesses and cultures).

Issues range from legally unacceptable discrimination, through addictions and complex medical conditions, to positive or negative, often subconscious, psychological reaction by the CV reader or recruiter.

I will express my thoughts directly, and these may prove in conflict with some politically correct views. That's tough! We live in a real world. There is no doubt that some political correctness is there to enforce just decisions and decent behaviours by employers and colleagues. But that is not always the case and political correctness can become unbalanced and harmful to normal behaviours.

In my opinion the way to approach most thorny issues is to be open and direct, but clever and intelligent. In some cases a mature judgement is needed. Above all be aware of what is important to an employer and what is not. The main criterion is whether or not the issue is likely to affect performance on the job.

Normally people reading CVs like to know that the writer is:

Honest;

Physically able to do the job without problems;

Mentally able to work in the organisation community without creating problems;

Stable in personality and with behaviours which do not create problems at work or at home,

Free of serious addictions like alcohol, drugs etc: these can create not only disturbance but also serious health and safety problems.

A major current practice by recruiting employers is pre-employment screening. It has been mentioned elsewhere that a gap in employment of more than two weeks is subject to positive referencing by the banking, government and other sectors. The systems used will pick up most concealed or omitted information.

Thorny issues may include:

Long period off due to illness

Past illness *fully recovered* would not, and does not, need to be mentioned, unless it caused a long period off work

Ongoing illness of a substantial kind needs to be declared.

Redundancy or having been fired

Redundancy is a fact of life, nowadays very common and not in itself a negative. It should generally be mentioned.

I often find myself advising how to deal with being fired from a job or leaving a job in unsatisfactory circumstances. My advice is to spend quite a bit of time formulating a *concise, accurate but upbeat two short sentences* enabling you to explain what happened in a confident and easy manner, and in truthful and clear words that will satisfy the interviewer and not invite further questions.

Life is not always fair and even being fired can have mitigating circumstances. But being fired for misconduct is something quite different and will be hard to explain away.

A long period off work for reasons like having a family

Long periods off for, e.g., having a family is totally legitimate and should be explained casually and *positively* in the CV.

A long time getting a new job

Time between jobs is again a fact of life. As already mentioned some sectors require documented evidence of the circumstances of a gap in employment. A significant gap should be mentioned in the CV and leaving documentation should always be kept for the positive referencing. Concise words to explain what happened (or didn't) are appropriate.

Time off for studying or travelling

Time off for studying or travelling is a legitimate part of personal development and should be briefly explained in a *positive* way.

Criminal record

Whether or not to declare a criminal record depends on its seriousness. If long past, best not to mention. If recent, you have to be up front and positive about it. If the tariff is not spent, it is legally necessary to declare it.

Medical conditions or incidents: stroke, heart attack, diabetes, asthma, epilepsy etc

Information on medical incidents and general health matters – as opposed to disability – will usually be required prior to employment.

Often these are best left until it looks as if an offer may be coming: get the firm to want you first. Then when you mention the condition, if it is past you can reassure them; if it is not, you will have a problem because it has to be declared. A long period off work due to illness will need to be explained in the CV unless it is several years past.

Mental illness

A particularly difficult issue is a mental illness which remains with you. This may range from a mild personality disorder to disorders which may create more serious problems with colleagues, customers etc. I feel it is best left to one's own judgement on whether and when to declare these. The answer will depend on, among other things, the conspicuousness of the problem.

Addiction to drugs or alcohol – past or current

Addictions affecting health and safety are serious for an employer. Major engineering organisations for example often require medical tests for these, and rules about drinking during working hours are rigorously upheld. These are seriously difficult problems to handle. As these addictions are self-imposed as well as medically complex, I do not propose to touch further on them here.

In my opinion, in many but not all of these there will be a moral obligation to declare the issue. In some it may be legitimate and appropriate not to declare the problem in a CV but to wait until an interview has been invited. In others it may be appropriate to mention the issue in a covering letter, when perhaps only the person opening the letter or email will see it.

In issues such as continuing illness, criminal record, ongoing personality disorder or addiction affecting H&S, the only comment I feel I can usefully make is similar to that of declaring one's age: one cannot change it so one must live with it. One must then create a state of mind in which one finds the most positive approach one can summon up, and be as positive as possible about the bad experience. You can say openly, for example, 'I have learned really useful lessons about how to interface effectively with people from this experience.' (Then you must be prepared to substantiate this statement.)

Discrimination is a different area. It can for example be based on age, gender, class, race, colour, education, physical handicap, sexual orientation, mental handicap, religion, past or present illness, etc. There are so many possible bases for discrimination that to try to hedge against all of them becomes ridiculous and produces the CV of a coward who cannot face up to the realities of the world.

A final general comment: be positive in every word and every line of your CV. <u>Any</u> negativity will eliminate you and the CV will be binned.

Chapter 11

Interpreting advertisements

A LOT CAN BE said on this, but it is a matter for basic intelligence.

Read the advertisement meticulously, word by word, with every bit of intelligence, insight, briefing, prior knowledge and imaginative thinking you can muster. See what the words actually say or imply about this job, this company, this organisation – and how the CV should be presented.

As in so much of what this book is about, what will make the critical difference in every case is how much you really want the job: and therefore how much thought, care and analysis you put into every step. In a competitive world, just wanting it is just not enough. If someone else wants it passionately and has self-belief in his or her ability to get it, then a half-hearted approach will get you nowhere.

Gleaning clues from the advertisement is a critical part of the process.

Chapter 12

Briefing on the company

ANY JOB FOR which you are applying and for which you are sending in a CV merits some investigation into the company. This is usually easy these days with the internet.

Wherever possible, get some personal input from a friend or acquaintance in the company: on what's going on in the organisation, and in particular this bit of the organisation – its strengths and weaknesses, commercial and financial performance, internal values and style.

But use any information you glean about the company with care. Do not overplay it in the CV, accompanying letter or interview. Always remember that asking questions is a very good way to display professional insight – without seeming to make out you know the answers to questions that you don't know.

Overplaying information about someone else's company and organisation runs the risk that your information on it may be wrong or not relevant to the part of the organisation you are going for. The company doesn't want solutions to problems it doesn't have – or doesn't think it has.

Chapter 13

Keywords

THESE ARE CRITICAL at all levels. Of course a well-written CV is actually a series of keywords anyway!

At the top level the selection of the words used in the CV is a crucial part of the creative process. At top levels most CVs will be handled entirely manually in all parts of the selection process, but will still be scanned by computer for tracking and record purposes.

From senior manager level downwards, keywords become increasingly important.

There are two forms of keyword in the context of a CV.

One is the wording within the text of the CV, which is picked up by automatic computer processing. Important types of keyword are:

Technical: electrical, mechanical, sales, accounting, buying, traction power, SAP, KPIs, retail, lighting, civil engineering, bridge building, M&E, project management, etc.

Industry/sector/specific company names: banking, cement, aerospace, tourism, Barclays, RBS, BAe etc.

The second is a list of selected keywords in a section, normally at the end of the CV, aimed at both computer-based analysis and at communicating specific skills to the technical recruiter.

Firing off a salvo of semi-random words is never as effective as carefully selected words defining a mix of technical, technical development, application, project, people-related experience etc.

Again, each CV is a different response to a specific requirement. Sometimes in a newspaper or web advertisement a specific format will be demanded. Sometimes you will know or will have found out about the company and its work. In all cases, the more *intelligent, insightful and clearly displayed* the keyword list is, as in every other part of the CV, the better will be the chance of getting that interview.

It is essential to put key *dimensions* in every section of the career story: numbers managed, £ or $ direct responsibility, significant achievements in sales, contract size, growth, profitability etc.

There is one further twist to the keyword tale. It is common practice for a recruiting employer to pose, say, three Killer Questions (KQs). These might be:

Do you have the right to work in Europe?

Do you have experience of managing multi-discipline teams?

Are you a chartered engineer?

KQs always have a one-word YES/NO answer. And if the text of the CV does not provide confirmation of each answer the computer will reject the CV: and the writer will not get the interview.

Part 2

The psychological foundation for careers and CVs

Chapter 14

The psychological foundation for writing CVs: some basic guidelines and thoughts

The first part of this book has been about pragmatic aspects of writing a CV, enabling you to compete with others in getting an interview.

Before you can write a winning CV you have to be in a positive and assertive – hopefully winning (!) – frame of mind. Even if the job you are applying for is a step up or into a new business sector or with new levels of responsibility, there must be an assertive confidence underlying your approach. Added to this, you need an open-minded exertion of intelligence to create out of your own self and experience something dynamic, interesting, relevant and exciting. Rehashing the same old ground and your preconceived, un-re-thought-out view of yourself will get you nowhere.

A further trap into which a surprisingly large number of people fall is a reluctance to *sell* themselves or talk about personal achievements. You are in competition with people wanting the same interview, the same job that you want. To be unwilling to get out there and sell yourself, what you are, what you can give, what you have given and achieved, and what you have to offer, displays some kind of psychological deficiency. How on earth can a brilliant candidate who thinks it is infra dig to sell ever win against a second-rate candidate who is a brilliant salesperson? Where does this sense of 'it's beneath me to sell' come from? Selling is one of the most demanding and exciting activities in the world, and is in any case a prerequisite for senior and leadership positions.

Remember that now much professional interviewing is based on situational and behavioural methods. Your CV should, if you want to win, lead the interviewer to pick up successes or actions that will display your winning characteristics and behaviours.

A CV not underwritten by mental attitude with such a desire to win simply will not win against an identical career history with winning attitude.

This opens up a huge area of thinking and many topics. Like,

> What is a manager's personality and makeup?
> Have I got it?
> Am I a leader, should I be going for leadership jobs?
> Do I know what I want to accomplish by my next career move?
> What actually am I, professionally and personally?
> What winning messages and behaviours do I have and how do I project them?

The core message of this section is *clarity of thinking*. About you, your winning attributes and behaviours, your past successes and wins, jobs, companies, why you want to move, will the move be the best one for you, where do you want to get to ...?

As with so much of this book, I feel I am preaching either to the converted or to the unconvertable – the unconvertable being people who will not or cannot understand. However, there must be some people in between whom these pages might stimulate into new thoughts, new effort or new directions in thinking.

Let's go back to square one. We are – most of us – steeped in our own life history and view it as a self-evident stream of events and developments. We tell the story over and over again using the same words and the same ideas. Our brain builds its own tramlines.

Of course it all matters to us, but we do not often stop to think that only particular aspects of it might be of interest to other people in particular circumstances.

The 'other people' might for example want to hear a different story if you want to join an Olympic egg and spoon race or seek a job as chairman of a defence company. The point is that serious focused thinking is needed to work out *a new and relevant way to tell the story of one's self and experience*, in the context of getting a job. This thinking will affect not just the writing of the CV and what you make it look like, but also what jobs you will apply for, what jobs you will make maximum effort to get, and how to conduct yourself, talk and behave at interviews.

What is a manager?

Without attempting to imitate thousands of books on this subject, one can usefully summarise key generic qualities sought by people recruiting managers:

Professionally, the competencies needed will normally include:

Business skills: what is your track record?

> General management, P&L, board membership, business strategy, generating successful business, restoring profitability, strategic planning, multifunctional management, financial and accounting management and strategy, organisation structures, business information.

Leadership skills: what is your track record?

> Do people naturally follow you? Have you a track record of taking an organisation or a group of people in genuinely new directions, or genuinely out of sticky situations?

Managing people: what is your track record?

> How many people, what kind and skill level, with what level of responsibility for delivering results and with what success? Hiring, firing, training, mentoring and developing people, succession planning, managing and developing work values and culture.

Organising skills: what is your track record?

> Are you organised yourself, are you effective at organising events, other people, situations, plans, projects, £MM programmes of work?

Organisation skills: what is your track record?
> Have you set up, managed, changed or led the structure and role of an organisation: if so on what scale/level?

Change management: what is your track record?
> Have you managed significant change and with what success?

Accounting and budget management: what is your track record and on what scale?
> Multicurrency, GAAP, expenditure control, management accounting.

Commercial skills: what is your track record?
> Sales, sales management, contract negotiation, contact management, customer relations, purchasing/buying/sourcing.

Functional skills: what is your track record?

Hiring managers will often take the view that with so many qualified candidates to choose from, they can't afford the time or the risk of looking at – let alone taking on – someone without both a strong generic skill set and direct relevant experience of what the job needs to be done.

You can also add to the impact of your CV with comments about working in outstanding organisations – commercially, in work culture, values, dynamic, creativity etc.

Personally, the attributes which are generic and desirable in people in senior positions include:

Personal substance
> Things like reliability, consistency, visible honesty, a good mind, openness in discussion and attitudes.

Values
> Integrity, behaviours towards other people which engender respect and response.

Personal authority
> Leadership, behaviours which engender respect for decisions and discussion, and lead to appropriate response and action.

Quality of mind

Traditional intelligence, but also what is called emotional intelligence – balance in the face of challenge or difficulty. Simple intelligence is two-a-penny: brilliance of mind with an inability to cope in 'real-life' people situations is of little interest (we say 'All brain and no brain').

Self-knowledge on these matters is critical. Where are you seriously strong or seriously weak? Your attributes and particular strengths can be communicated through the story you tell in your CV and at interview.

Remember that 'track record' is everything. It shows what you are and what you aren't and if you cannot show a track record, don't try to pretend that you have an attribute that you cannot substantiate. 'Situation interviews' are very common, and if you cannot substantiate an attribute you claim, you will be shown up.

The natural next step in this logic is to think about what the areas are where you know you are not at the top level, and what the areas are where you want to strengthen your expertise.

A serious weakness or gap in your experience is quite different from an area where you want to gain experience as part of personal/professional development. The latter can be clearly expressed and is purposeful. The former need not be revealed unless it is a real issue in the selection process.

For example, you would not normally apply for a sales manager's job if you have never done actual selling yourself. But suppose you had done marketing and production or R&D on a highly specialist product and wished to broaden into general management in this specialist field. Then you could be open about your lack of sales experience but would counter this with your unique knowledge of the product, markets, applications, relevant science etc; and your personality and ability to interact well with people and customers; and how this would make you an effective salesperson; and you want very much to acquire this skill to help you move into general management …

Career strategy and strategic thinking

The more senior the position, or the more ambitious the candidate, the more strategic thinking ability is valued. Top level headhunters or managers will often consider that good strategic thinking about one's career indicates good business strategic thinking ability.

What is strategic thinking? It is the thinking process which defines short-, medium- and longer-term direction, integrates everything affecting and affected by this direction, and ensures that all short-term actions and relevant decisions down the track are made to be consistent with the strategy. Thus strategic thinking is about

- Direction
- Integrating multifaceted information
- Making links between different issues
- Setting priorities
- Seeing the wood for the trees, not getting bogged down in detail
- Cutting out irrelevant information

Strategic thinking about your career should be reflected in the way your CV is written, as well as in choice of job applications and conduct at interviews.

Ask questions, such as:
- What is going to be the best next move for me?
- Is this job really a good move, and why?
- How is it relevant to my short- and longer-term aims?
- Does it fit my personal development plan?

Eliminate superfluous information such as minor details of education and training, specific dates when you started and ended specific jobs (as opposed to employment with a company).

Include significant landmarks in your career, in responsibilities entrusted to you, in your personal and professional development.

Be very clear in expressing what you want next, where you want your career to take you and how this job fits that.

Try to make your CV express steady personal growth.

This thinking should give the CV describing your career a completely different look. You will find yourself using different words, new ideas, saying different things, referring to different facts, and presenting achievements in a different way.

Now about yourself

As well as re-thinking *what* you say about your career and professional life to the outside world, *how* you say it and *why*, you can similarly develop insights into and new observations about your personal self. This may result in a change in how you think about yourself; it should colour your CV and presentation of yourself in subtle but real ways.

Too many people think the personal self has no place in a CV. They couldn't be more wrong. The essence of many appointments is finding a candidate who has the personal substance to last the course, can be trusted, will keep things running sweetly when the boss is away, will not cause the upsets all managers can do without – and at the top levels will provide the leadership and discipline which delivers the corporate results.

Once again, it must be emphasised that the difference is subtle – but enough to differentiate the CV of someone who has done the thinking from someone with an identical career who hasn't.

The types of personal attributes listed above, described as generic attributes, were:

Personal substance
Values
Personal authority
Quality of mind

These should all somehow be visible in the way the story is told in the CV. One reason for listing them is that they can act as pointers to more self-knowledge about your strengths and weaknesses.

This knowledge can in turn direct you towards or away from particular jobs or firms.

There are further reasons for adding information about your personal attributes:

> Carefully selected factual information about you will give a picture of what sort of person you are and how you balance your work and private life.
>
> In my opinion most political correctness has little usefulness in business. Age and date of birth for example: leave them out and it gives an impression of fear about whatever it might be, and age is easily roughly guessed, anyway.
>
> Sports information is relevant if it represents a real achievement such as endurance, leadership or performance at an extreme level. If a current job for example does not have a high leadership content but you are leader of a mountain rescue team, point out the leadership demands of the non-work role.
>
> Membership of bodies or councils is significant if it demonstrates broader interests, achievements, bestowed responsibilities, or a position of respect in a trade or public position. Pick out what matters and present your role in it.
>
> The simple sentence: 'Won Sword of Honour at Dartmouth', or 'Captain of university rugby' or 'Led expedition to climb Mt Kilimanjaro for charity' speaks volumes.
>
> However to put in a CV, for example, 'following Spurs on TV' is the biggest yawn. And if you write a CV which for every role says something like: 'I was highly commended for my work in this position' then 'I succeeded beyond expectations' then 'I successfully ...' then 'this work received high praise' (I often get these), it is so revealing about your substance and character as to eliminate you with a gasp of irritation as the scrumpled CV hits the bin.
>
> If you haven't got anything significant to say on a topic, don't try to find something for the sake of it. Keep everything you do say sharp, short, relevant and really interesting.

When you have done all this thinking

Now you can sit down to write your CV. While doing this you will

- Learn what words accurately describe you, your capabilities.
- Review how to describe your experience – personal and professional – in the most concise and effective way, eliminating every superfluous word and leaving the bare bones of what really counts. This will also be a critical piece of preparation for interviews.
- Plan how you will put over your personal attributes, qualities and experiences through the way you tell the story.
- Assess how relevant any job is to you, how much you want to go for it.
- Mould your CV and thinking to the job – and the industry, the sector, the company – and its culture, markets, technology, products, external business challenges, internal organisation challenges, etc. Respond to any clues given in an advertisement as to what they really want.

Then you can refine the cv you have created and make it look beautiful, with style and clarity, all the time remembering that:

- You are in competition with umpteen other people who want the job as much as you;
- many of them are likely to be as well qualified as you;
- many of them will have attributes you don't have (and of course vice versa); and
- *only those with the most outstanding and relevant CVs will get the interviews.*

And what will make a CV outstanding?

The quality and depth of thought that goes into writing it.

Chapter 15

A final summary and check list

A CV should be cleverly put together, so that:

Visually it makes The Reader feel this person has *style, dynamic, creativity and thinks well of himself or herself*. Not with reams of words crammed into a page; use modern typeface, wide margins, avoid small font.

It displays personal and professional *substance*, achievement and attributes, demonstrates ability to contribute commercially (or in whatever way matters to The Reader) and is interesting.

It takes full account of the requirements of *computer processing* and the need for the computer to pick out key facts and information.

Personal attributes and virtues emerge from the facts. Comments about one's experience or virtues are never read: they are *always* seen as wishful thinking, self-promoting lies or thoughtless jingles.

Its *concise and clear thinking* shows The Reader that this person is not a bore, realises the Reader's time is short, and is not someone who wants tediously to talk about his or her point of view and achievements.

It is *forward looking*: nothing you've done is of any interest to The Reader except insofar as it shows you can solve his or her problems in the future.

Its layout enables The Reader to see *in 5 seconds* whether to be *interested* and read the rest.

It *avoids detail* readers do not need to know. If they are interested they will find out.

It tells a story. Bullet points are (in my view) an ineffective way of doing so. They make the document boring.

It communicates. Remember, *communication is not what is said but what is heard*. So the document must cause a calculated impact on The Reader's mind: to do that means knowing what that impact is meant to be.

Shortness is not a particular virtue especially when it raises more questions than it answers. But with a bit of *effort*, most aspects of a career and personality can be expressed in *two pages*, occasionally three.

A *slapdash CV* which has taken less than 10–20 hours to write will almost invariably result in *being binned* when in competition with CVs which are better prepared.

The CV is not and never will be 'the way to achieve the career job of your dreams', as is claimed in some books on CVs. The CV is one building block towards it – but a critical one. The CV is a product of a total state of mind, attitude and being.

Part 3

Examples of CVs and how to improve them

Two very different sample CVs on the model described

then

Extracts of real CVs from the last 7–8 years, followed by some re-writing in the style described in the book.

The print in the following pages is reduced in size to enable the CVs to fit into the number of pages when done in typescript

Example 1 of full CV

Xbbb Bxxx

99 Jonas Grove, Onetwo, County CO10 0BD, 078XX SSS CCC
xbbb.bxxx@hotmail.com

Dob 1st April 1969 (42) Married, x children

Group Sales & Marketing Director of a £450m service business
Dynamic, high integrity leader and developer of people
Advanced commercial and business skills
Ready for a board level general management job

Education etc

Commissioned at RAF Cranwell, attended Staff College
BTEC Business Studies, Harvard Business School Leadership Program
Fellow Institute of Sales & Marketing; extensive sales, sales management and commercial training

Career

2005 – present   CLEANLY SERVICE GROUP LTD, XXXX PLC
£450m market leading service group, UK division of £bn XXXX Group. In these years Cleanly has grown £300-450m, its markets, organisation and technologies changed dramatically and it made significant acquisitions.

2007 – present   Group Sales & Marketing Director reporting to Cleanly Service Group CEO.

A new role to plan and lead radical changes, & integrate businesses across healthcare, aaaa solutions, & direct/web channels. Key aims:
  Initiate & drive new marketing-led business strategies, build cross-selling and break down silo mentalities, improve interfaces between Operations, Sales & Service, sort out legacy problems in acquired businesses.

Key activities and achievements:
  Led strategies producing £100m sales growth in 3 years, Led reviews & BPR in medical, hospitality & other sectors Built cross-divisional sales & sharing of best practice, Created a Group Sales Leadership Programme & new incentives, Introduced sector sales & marketing; led strategic accounts, Personally coached sales directors, MDs & managers, Renewed Cleanly brand image & core values, Member of Group Strategic Review resulting in radical reshaping.

Personally developed from a division sales director into a business leader.

2005–07   Sales Director – bbbb Division – old-fashioned £220m core business of Cleanly. Reports: 6 Regional Sales Managers with 65 Sales Execs, 69 Customer

Account Managers, and National Account Sales Director. Addressed the need for change. Created a new dynamic sales culture and organisation, new pricing and commercial strategies and new commission structure; opened up web and direct sales. Achieved 7 sales records.

2004–2005   HARDWARE LTD – CONSTRUCTION MATERIALS GROUP

Regional Sales Director with 7 ASMs, 6 KAMs, 1 Regional Sector Manager, 104 external sales reps. Responsible for sales, margin & marketing strategy of 130 branches. Sales budget £337m. Personally accountable for top 20 customers and suppliers. Achieved highest performing team.

2002–2004   QFREIGHT (GB) LTD

National Sales Training Director. Led new training programmes. Managed major accounts & generated £650k new business in first year. Recruited and trained 20 new staff & regional managers.

2002   COLD FOOD DISTRIBUTION

Nordic temperature-controlled logistics Head of Commercial. Member of UK board, appointed to reorganise sales, commercial & marketing. Achieved much in a short time.

1999–2002   GEORGIE UNITED DISTRIBUTION

French supply chain logistics

2001–02   Sales & Marketing Director. Restructured UK sales operations, led an international sales team, achieved new commercial results.

1999–01   NSM with 5 RSMs, 42 sales execs, 5 contract managers. Achieved double target. Provided new training. Appointed 'Change Agent'.

1999   RSM. Won Sales Manager of the Month 6 times in 10 months.

1998–1999   PARCELINE Senior Sales Exec.

1997–1998   WICKSTEED LEISURE LTD Area Sales Manager.

1988–1997   ROYAL AIR FORCE Commissioned, Flight Lieutenant, Air Traffic Controller.

PERSONAL

Time with family. Charity challenges – abseiling down waterfalls, buildings; 90-mile hike in 4 days, team motor challenges. Preferred charities: Starlight, Marie Curie. Sub-Aqua diving (qualified member of BSAC). Most outdoor sports esp motor sport.

Example 2 of full CV

Sir Xxxx Xxxx KCB, OBE
The Fields, xxxx Road, xxxx Heath, xxxx, SS1 1SS
07xxx xxx xxx, 01xxxx xxxxxx (home), xxxx.xxxx@xxxx.com
DoB: 16 June 19xx (xx) Married, 4 children.

Vice Admiral, Deputy Commander-in-Chief Fleet
Leader-manager, exceptional people skills, independent mind
Able to take strategic & difficult decisions; tested in war
Former nuclear submarine commander
At 57, seeking a new career and new life challenges

I have rare and international experience: in command, operational planning & management, advice at ministerial level, big project management, large budgets, negotiation and diplomacy, and strategic thinking aimed at <u>winning</u>.

My search for new challenges could take me in several directions: for example national functions, large projects, marine operations, or non-executive board positions. I bring exceptional personal and professional qualities, competencies, analytical skills, open-mindedness and sense of strategy.

Education and personal development

20xx Advanced Management Achievement Course, xxxx BS
20xx Senior Managers' Financial Seminar, London BS
20xx US DoD strategic course
19xx UK Higher Command & Staff Course (MoD top command course)
19xx Joint Services Defence College (MSc level political & strategic studies)
19xx Graduated from Dartmouth (1st Degree level)

Career History

20xx – present **Deputy Commander-in-Chief Fleet** (Vice Admiral)
Commanding RN's front-line operations worldwide. One of three officers qualified and on call to command 50,000 UK forces in multi-national operations worldwide, heading a 1,200-strong deployable HQ. Organised xxxx Fleet Review involving massive security and negotiations across government agencies.

Led design and implementation of a major strategic change programme, completed 2 years early, saved xx staff and £yym pa. Made the HQ organisation the place people aspire to join.

20xx–xx **Assistant Chief of Naval Staff** (Rear Admiral)
Equivalent to Chief Executive of the Navy. Member of Admiralty Board chaired by Secretary of State for Defence. Resource budget £2bn, assets £18bn and employing 40,000 people.

Led project to rationalise RN organisation to reduce bureaucracy. Member of team reducing MoD Head Office numbers by xxx.

20xx **Commander International Task Group** (Captain)
Commanded Task Group (2,000 people) on a round-the-world deployment to boost government and industry interests.

Led political, operational and sales activity in 32 cities. Achieved all international and national objectives; exceeded commercial expectations of defence industry in demonstration events. Built relationships with senior politicians and military leaders of countries visited. Operated with 17 different navies. Developed methods and procedures still in use.

Built a strong & vibrant team able to deal with any eventuality. Responsible for planning, administration, maintenance, safety, morale and welfare. Motivated personnel throughout long period away from home without losing a single day's operation, and with no major accidents or injuries.

19xx – 20xx **Deputy Flag Officer Submarines**
Responsible for day-to-day operation of the UK's submarine fleet.

Instigated and led radical change in the Submarine Service management structure.

19xx **Deputy Assistant Chief of Staff** (xxxx Division)
Member of new tri-service HQ to command all UK operations worldwide. Set up HQ in half allocated three months. Moulded Navy, Army, RAF and civil servants into strongly bonded, fiercely proud and admired team.

1984 – 1997 Earlier Command Appointments included

1993. HMS XXXX (frigate). Led embargo operations against Yugoslavia; ship was awarded Sword of Peace for her work in Albania.
1989. HMS XXXX (nuclear-powered attack submarine). Led 4 arduous 'Cold-War' patrols, mostly beneath arctic ice cap. Appointed OBE.
1987. Commanded international course for specially selected officers, qualifying them to be submarine commanding officers.
1983. HMS XXXX (diesel submarine). Designed and successfully introduced methods to insert and recover Special Forces, still in use.
1982. HMS XXXX (nuclear-powered attack submarine). Second in command. Fully tested under the stresses of the Falklands War.

Other

Vice-President of RN Football. Member of the Institute of Directors.
Freeman of the City of London.

Example 3: improvements to parts of real CVs

Original version

Jan 96 – April 99 Position: General Manager Middle East and Africa

The role carries overall responsibility for the operational performance of the countries in the region with specific focus on strategy and the maximising of market share growth of mobile communications products and the management of the following functions:

Sales	Marketing	Operations
Service	Finance	

During the last few years the operation has gone through a period of rapid growth and has a significant multi-million $ turnover. It operates in over 30 countries in the region through an extensive distribution network (Network Operators, Distributors and Dealers) with local offices located in the UAE, South Africa and the UK.

Member of the management board for the Middle East and Africa region.

Key Achievements:

Exceeding key targets, growing market share in the region and developing a profitable operation. The group was returned to a profit position at the end of 1996.

Establishing the Middle East and Africa Organisation and developing an effective remote team. Three years ago there was no established organisation in the region.

Created and implemented the distribution strategy for the region.

Developed and executed successful new product and new market entry strategies. Driving change programmes i.e. centralised fulfilment centre, in country service operations.

Strengthening the brand of xxxxxx in the region.

Suggested improved version of the same

1996-99 General Manager Middle East and Africa, member of region management board. 30 countries, 75 staff in offices in UK, UAE, S Africa & UK, and multinational distribution through Network Operators, Distributors and Dealers. Responsible for delivering new organisation, increased market share and profit. Directly responsible for £267m revenue and 75 staff reports: Sales, Marketing, Operations, Finance, Service.

    Created/implemented from scratch:
        new region organisation and culture;
        new region distribution strategy;
        new product and market entry strategies;
        new centralised fulfilment centre;
        in-country service operations.

    Exceeded key targets; grew market share,
    Restored profitability by end of first year.
    Created major brand presence in the region.

This version

Has 20 lines instead of 32
Has 103 words instead of 211
Is clearer, punchy and concise with quantitative data
Is visually easy to absorb with key points emphasised

Note: Figures are not derived from the original but are given as examples

Example 4: improvements to parts of real CVs

Original version – extract from CV

Profile:

A senior PROGRAMME and PROJECT manager with over 20 years commercial experience including working within Blue Chip companies. John has proven senior management, technology and business skills operating at Business, compliance, IT, Commercial, and Programme levels across management, strategic & consultancy roles to ensure both compliance and commercial focus and delivery.

In recent years, John has led a number of business critical programmes with high technology and compliance content. In his current assignment he has been responsible for the delivery of a regulated business environment ahead of new FSA regulations for the mortgage industry. Previously, he led a programme of over 400 people on a major E-COMMERCE implementation with a budget of £250M that crossed diverse business areas and technical platforms.

John has been successful in a number of different business environments and organisational structures. Whilst recognising the realities and constraints of modern business, John has always been able to enable business success through the use of innovative technical solutions and he has a breadth of experience in a variety of technologies.

John has been able to leverage formal methodologies such as PRINCE to ensure a controlled and consistent delivery of both business and technical products. He has a clear understanding of financial issues both in the project and across the business in general. He is pragmatic in his application of methodology and strives to ensure that it is applied sensibly.

He is adept at working closely with project, business and technical stakeholders and recognises the needs of each. He is an effective problem solver and achieves success by balancing business objectives against the art of the possible.

Programme & Project Experience:

Dec 2003 to date		Programme Manager	xxxx
2003 – Dec 2003	7 Months	Development / Test Project Manager	vvvv LOGISTICS
2002 – 2003	8 Months	Programme Manager	zzzz IT SOLUTIONS
2002 – 2002	6 Months	Programme / Delivery Manager	(wwww Plc)
2000 – 2002	2 Years	Programme Manager, Project Manager Delivery Manager, Test Manager, Release Manager	cccc (nnnnnnn Plc)
1999 – 2000	1 Year	Programme Manager	bbbb
1998 – 1999	1 Year	Project Manager	vvvv
1995 – 1998	3 Years	Project/Programme Manager	jjjj
1993 – 1998	5 Years	Project/Programme Manager	Ttttt, ppppp, hhhh

Areas of Expertise:

- Project Management (10+ Years)
- Delivery Management (10+ Years)
- Programme Management (10+ Years)
- Strategic Management (10+ Years)
- Team Management & Team Building (10+ Years)
- Test Management (10+ Years)
- Release Management (10+ Years)
- Management of Relationships to Board Level (18 Years)
- Technical/Business Communication at all levels (20 Years)
- Resource Management (18 Years)
- Single and concurrent, multiple projects management and delivery (10+ Years)
- Integration Management
- PRINCE2 (5 Years)
- Stakeholder Management (10+ years)
- Outsourcing management & delivery (5 Years)
- Direct budgetary responsibility (18 Years)
- Delivery of application support models (10+ Years)
- Service Level Agreements (SLA's) (10+ Years)
- Management of 3rd Party suppliers (18 Years)
- Delivery of revenue and profit to targets (18 Years)
- Problem Management (18 Years)
- Commercial focus (20 Years)
- Comprehend and deliver to business imperatives (20 Years)
- E-Commerce

Qualifications:

- HND/HNC Computer Science APU Cambridge

Career History

xxxx (Subsidiary of the nnnnnnnnnn Building Society) – MPoS/ aaaa (Systems) + FSA Regulation Programme (2003 – Oct 31) System & Regulation Programme (SRP 1 Nov 04 to date)

Project Methodology: Prince2

bbbb Home Loans is a wholly owned subsidiary of llll Building Society that provides one of the widest self-certification product ranges available in the market, including Residential and Buy to Let investment mortgages. They are currently ranked the No 1 Self Cert lender in the market.

In October 2004, the FSA regulation for mortgage lending came into force, without a doubt the largest and most pervasive single change that the mortgage industry has seen. Although part of llll, bbbb is a separate operating entity and decided to seek FSA certification independent of their parent. In 2003 a programme of work was initiated to ensure compliance across all business areas against the October 2004/5 deadline. At the same time, it was deemed that it would be too expensive and impractical to make the front and back office systems compliant. The decision was taken to adopt the llll systems for sales and administration.

John was brought into UCB as the Regulation & MPoS/aaaa (System) Programme Manager. His brief was to ensure compliance in all areas of the organisation in readiness for the deadline. In this role John had responsibility for all business change and also took on board the move to the new system and the business changes associated with that.

During this Programme, John had direct responsibility for 31 separate and diverse workstreams. He had a team of 35 people and indirect responsibility of 60+ more across the business who worked as part of his team as required.

The success of the Programme has been recognised by bbbb who have hailed it as 'the biggest challenge we ever met'.

Following on from his successful management of the FSA compliance programme, John was asked to head up the newly-formed Systems and Regulation Programme (SRP) to continue in developing processes and systems to further enhance bbbb's ability to offer best-in-sector service to its clients and to ensure ongoing regulatory compliance. The SRP encompasses both systems and procedures to help bbbb maintain its business standing and regulation both in terms of FSA compliance and Sarbanes-Oxley, Basel II compliance.

Responsibilities include:

• Programme Management	• Plan and monitor the projects (31 project)
• Direct and motivate the project teams	• Knowledge Transfer
• Risk Management	• Integration planning
• Issue Management	• Mentoring
• Programme Office	• Stakeholder management
• Resource Management	

Technologies include:	**Commercial Areas:**
• Bespoke Nationwide Systems (MPoS ALIAS etc)	• Mortgages
• ICL	• FSA Regulatory
• AS400 mainframe	• Financial
• SQL Server databases	• Web both b2b & b2c
• Web	• Insurance

Suggested improved version

Major IT programme manager: up to £250m involving 400 staff
Has _delivered_ major programmes in several business sectors
Expert in project methodologies, Prince etc
Resolves people, stakeholder and technical demands
Balances business, IT, compliance & commercial need

Technical overview: 20 years managing and delivering major IT programmes, as leader, line manager and consultant. I have a good track record of delivery meeting budget and time targets. Proven senior management, technology and business skills: delivering Business, Compliance, IT, Commercial, and Programme objectives. I have achieved this in E-commerce in financial and logistics sectors; have exercised leadership of organisation change and management of stakeholder needs and expectation. Can balance business objectives vs the art of the possible.

Keywords: Application: Direct and motivate project teams, knowledge transfer, plan monitor projects (up to 31), PRINCE, E-commerce, mortgage systems, insurance systems, logistics systems, FSA regulation, compliance, programme delivery and test, budget responsibility, SLAs, 3rd party suppliers, application support models, release management, management of relationships to board level, resource management, single/concurrent multiple projects management and delivery, integration management, team management & team building.

Keywords: Technical: Web both b2b & b2c, PRINCE, Bespoke Systems AS400 mainframe, ICL, SQL Server databases.

2003 – present   XXXX (Subsidiary of NNNN BUILDING SOCIETY)
Market leader in self-certification products including investment mortgages. In 2003 major new systems work was commenced to meet FSA regulations coming into force in 2004. Project methodology PRINCE 2.

2004 – present   Head of XXXX's newly formed Systems & Regulation Programme
Responsible for subsequent developments in systems and business procedures to ensure XXXX provides best-in-sector service to clients, and regulatory compliance with FSA and Sarbanes-Oxley Basel II. Promoted following success in delivering the previous programmes.

[Note that his version makes no reference to his responsibility for development strategies, reporting lines, staff numbers, budget responsibilities etc.]

2003–04 Programme Manager, MPoS/aaaa Systems and FSA Regulation Programme. Brief: ensure compliance in all areas of the organisation for the 2004 deadline, managing all system and related business change.

Direct responsibility for 31 separate workstreams, direct team of 35, and further resource of 60+ across the business as required.

The programme's success was recognised by the parent company as meeting 'the biggest challenge we ever had'.

[*Note that his version makes no reference to time and budget targets achieved, development strategies, etc. These are serious omissions*]

This version

Has 51 lines instead of 179
Has 345 words instead of 972
Is clearer, punchy and concise, with no boxes
Is visually easy to absorb with key points emphasised
And it shows how the sea of disorganised information in the original conceals how much important information has been left out

Example 5: improvements to parts of real CVs

Original version

Sales Director

PERSONAL PROFILE:

With many years experience in Sales and Operations I am now looking to progress my career in a forward thinking organisation, where I'm able to fully utilise my extensive skill set and can add considerable value, whilst continuing to develop a business and my own personal growth. Operationally strong, I adopt a flexible attitude, able to react quickly to challenges and demands.

I have a very broad understanding of the Sales environment and a full understanding of the commercial business, which I believe, enables me to be a successful business manager.

Relevant Experience

1. Proven sales background.
2. Strong financial management and able to exploit commercial opportunities in order to maximise sales.
3. Strong analytical skill set.
4. Passion and experience in to further develop and grow existing business
5. Experienced in leading Field Sales Managers and inspiring employees.
6. Deliver operational best practices & drive high performance
7. Delivery of major projects.
8. Good communicator with strong intellect, sound judgment.
9. Proven Leadership skills
10. Ability to foster a customer-centric culture

Key Strengths

1. A strategic-thinker, collaborative individual who's able to achieve results via influence and persuasion.
2. Strong emphasis on quality results and working effectively under pressure.
3. Determined attitude and drive & reach personal and organisational goals.
4. Able to react quickly to changes and demands.
5. Pro-active business leader with a pragmatic approach
6. Energetic and open management style
7. Business focused committed to exceeding
8. Able to gain credibility and trust to influence

CAREER HISTORY

Associate Sales Director   XXXX   January 2002 – September 2004

Fastest Growing Retailer of the year, last two years UK, £ 2billion operation with total employee base over 4,000, reporting directly to Managing Director with responsibility for sales and profitability's of 30 retail stores, direct reports consist of a strong field Structure; Area Sales Managers, Operations Managers, Training & Human Resources teams and Audit. Full control of P&L performance and increase all KPI's and maximise profit opportunities, responsible for £2m operating profit.

Achievements

1. Delivered profit and cost targets consistently month on month
2. Increased like for like sales by 30%, which is one of the highest in the company
3. Increased Business to Business sales by 40%
4. Successfully opened 9 new sites that exceeded net contribution budgets
5. Recruited and retained a highly motivated management team
6. Part of the Senior Team, making business decisions
7. Delivered 'Individual Performance Improvement Management' of all managers and staff
8. Introduction of compliance and operational standards
9. Introduction of new business strategies
10. Won several company incentives
11. Designed and implemented business enhancing process i.e. Store Visit criteria, new systems, review process

Suggested improved version of the same

Experienced, operationally strong retail sales director
Broad product experience in UK top retail majors
Strong commercial, negotiating and analytical skills
Responsive, inspiring leader of field sales with passion

I have had a successful sales career based on

- Good communication, thinking, judgement, strategy
- Leadership skills, getting results by influence, persuasion
- Fostering customer-centric attitudes
- Emphasis on quality results; delivering under pressure
- Determined attitude and drive
- Ability to react quickly to changes and demands
- Pro-active & pragmatic approach; energetic and open
- Ability to gain credibility and trust

Career

2002–2004/5 XXXX
Fastest-growing UK retailer of the year. £2bn, 4,000 employees.

Associate Sales Director reporting to Managing Director. Responsible for P&L, sales & KPIs of 30 retail stores with £2m operating profit. Reports: Area Sales Managers, Operations Managers, Training & HR & Audit. Member of the executive team. Achievements:

- Met profit, cost & KPI targets consistently month on month Introduced new business strategies: increased like for like sales by 30%, increased B2B sales 40%
- Opened 9 new sites, all exceeded net contribution budgets
- Recruited & retained a motivated management team
- Delivered performance improvement of all managers & staff
- Introduced compliance and operational standards
- Won several company incentives
- Designed and implemented business enhancing process i.e. store visit criteria, new systems, review process

This version

Has 37 lines instead of 58
Has 209 words instead of 446
Is clearer, punchy and concise: puts over the sales manager's vitality
Is visually easy to absorb with key points emphasised

Example 6: improvements to parts of real CVs

Original version

SSSS YYYY MBA (distinction) Chartered Marketer, MCIM, FIDM, MIoD
6, vvvv Gardens, cccc, Surrey KTxx 0vv. 078bbbbbbb ssssyyyy@aol.com

Strategic Marketing Director with significant expertise gained in senior roles with global FTSE and blue chip service organisations.

Key skills and achievements

- **Marketing & Communications:** Comprehensive knowledge of all marketing disciplines. Developed, launched and directed highly effective innovative marketing and commercial strategies, international brands, service propositions, channels, internal/external PR and PA campaigns, global website, database and CRM initiatives.

- **Strategic business development:** Leveraged global business relationships to maximise revenue achievement. Introduced M&A, business and product opportunities.

- **Change Management:** Experienced in business re-structuring and transformation environments. Influenced and implemented change programmes, developed new commercial models and strategic solutions to meet changing business needs.

- **Commercial acumen:** Delivered to target on multi-million pound revenue and cost responsibilities through ROI measurement, and ensured effective control of resource.

- **Relationship building:** Devised innovative CRM strategies and systems for successful and highly profitable loyalty programmes. Negotiated and launched new partnerships.

- **Inspirational leader:** Reorganised and developed marketing and customer service teams to achieve improved performance, productivity and increase value-add activities.

- **Excellent communicator:** Extensive experience in writing and delivering business presentations, reports, briefings and plans to audiences internationally at all levels.

Career History

HQ moved to Amsterdam

xxxx   October 2003 – December 2007

Director of Strategic Development and Marketing

Joined as Marketing Director for Initial Hygiene (£90m t/o UK business) and promoted within 5 months. Role reported into the Divisional Managing Director, a CEO direct report. The division represented circa 25% of the £2.9bn group turnover, comprising a number of market-leading B2B companies operating across multiple international sites. Joining this (formerly) sales-driven plc as the first ever professionally qualified marketer in the senior management team proved an exciting challenge. Encompassing all marketing and strategic management disciplines, it provided a broadening of experience and skills through exposure to a variety of business activities and situations. Carrying significant responsibility for the development of research-led marketing and strategic planning within the group, the role continuously shifted and evolved with the company's major re-structuring, disposal and acquisition activities. Major projects included:

- Directed the global launch and re-brand of new environmental service concept. Commissioned extensive targeted business research, initiated CRM systems, directed all marcomms activities and relationships to drive rapid adoption worldwide.

- Strategic research to create a multiple service UK market proposition, devised commercial models, made recommendations and prepared board presentations.

- Strategic assessment, identified market gaps and opportunities, providing recommendations for acquisition or disposal of businesses.

- Introduced customer profiling, segmentation and analytics, creating data driven strategies and highlighting need for massive data improvement and an ERP solution.

- Developed new positioning and brand essence for a major group brand.

- Member of international steering group formed to accelerate the implementation of new global/regional websites and develop the web as a major B2B channel.

- Undertook commercial reviews of businesses within the division, researching internal and external data and developing presentations to brief new Chief Executive Officer.

- Introduction of formal marketing planning, budgeting and ROI metrics.

- Directed a 14-month long communications programme to at-risk personnel and external customers in disposal/merger of 4 companies and worked closely with the MD to develop new business models (subsequently endorsed by Bain & Co)

- Completed major research project to devise a new market proposition and branding for a key service stream, now undergoing a global re-launch.

- Commissioned research, developed and launched new products and services.

Suggested improved version

SSSS YYYY

6, vvvv Gardens, cccc, Surrey KTxx 0vv. 078bbbbbbb ssssyyyy@aol.com

Education   MBA (distinction)

Qualifications Chartered Marketer, MCIM, FIDM, MIoD

Strategic Marketing Director in £500m & global service business
Commercial and business development track record
Advanced marketing, brand, CRM & communications expertise
People, leadership and change management skills

Career:

2003-2007   MAJOR UK SERVICE CO PLC

Joined as Marketing Director for bbbb Ltd, £90m UK business, part of a global business division.

After 5 months was promoted to Director of Strategic Development and Marketing of the global £700m division, made up of market-leading international B2B companies. Reported to Divisional Managing Director (direct report to £2.9bn Group CEO).

This was an exciting challenge: I was the first ever professional marketer in the senior management team of this previously sales-led business. My role encompassed all marketing, strategic management and strategic corporate planning disciplines, most set up from scratch: covering businesses serving many sectors in many countries and cultures. The role shifted and evolved as the company went through major re-structuring, disposal and acquisition activities. Projects included:

Directed worldwide launches & brand positioning of major service offerings.

Strategic market gap & opportunity analysis backed by research, commercial modelling; recommended acquisitions & disposals.

New approaches to business analysis and customer profiling; resulted in new data-driven methods, massive data improvement and major ERP solution.

Member of international steering group developing the web as major B2B channel & leading the introduction of new global/regional websites.

Conducted commercial reviews of businesses. Introduced M&A, business and product opportunities.

Introduced formal marketing planning, budgets, ROI metrics.

Directed a 14-month programme to keep at-risk personnel and external customers in the disposal/merger of 4 companies. Worked closely with the MD to develop new business models (endorsed by Bain & Co).

This version

Has 59 lines instead of 81
Has 293 words instead of 582
Is clearer, punchy and concise
Is visually easy to absorb with key points emphasised
Increases the sense of excitement
But even this version lacks much of the information any reader would want to know.